WOLOF

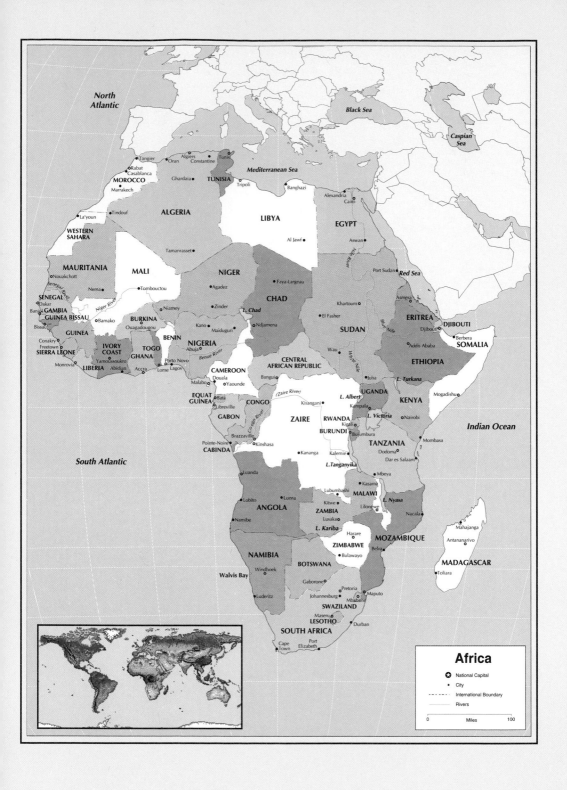

North
Atlantic

Black Sea

Caspian
Sea

Tangier
Rabat   Algiers Oran Constantine Tunis
Casablanca
MOROCCO   Ghardaia   TUNISIA   Tripoli   Banghazi
Marrakech

Mediterranean Sea

Alexandria
Cairo

La'youn   Tindouf

WESTERN
SAHARA

ALGERIA

LIBYA

EGYPT

Aswan

Tamanrasset

Al Jawf

Nile River

Port Sudan   Red Sea

MAURITANIA

MALI

NIGER

Nouakchott   Faya-Largeau
Nema   Agadez   CHAD   Khartoum   Asmera
Tombouctou   Asmera

Senegal River

Niger River   Niamey   Zinder   L. Chad   El Fasher   ERITREA   DJIBOUTI
DAKAR   Bamako   Kano   Ndjamena   Djibouti   Berbera
SENEGAL   BURKINA   Maiduguri   SUDAN   Addis Ababa   SOMALIA
Banjul GAMBIA   Ouagadougou
GUINEA BISSAU   BENIN   Wau   ETHIOPIA
Bissau   GUINEA   NIGERIA   White Nile   Juba   L. Turkana
Conakry   IVORY   Abuja   CENTRAL   Bangui
Freetown   COAST   TOGO   Benue River   AFRICAN REPUBLIC   UGANDA   Mogadishu
SIERRA LEONE   GHANA   Porto Novo   CAMEROON   L. Albert   KENYA
Monrovia   Yamoussoukro   Lome Lagos   Douala   Kisangani   Kampala   Nairobi
LIBERIA   Abidjan   Accra   Yaounde   (Zaire River)   L. Victoria
EQUAT.   Malabo   CONGO   RWANDA   Mombasa
GUINEA   Bata   ZAIRE   BURUNDI   Bujumbura
GABON   Libreville   Kigali   TANZANIA
Brazzaville   Dodoma
Pointe-Noire   Kinshasa   Kananga   Kalemie   Dar es Salaam
CABINDA   L.Tanganyika   Mbeya

South Atlantic

Luanda   Kasama
Lobito   Luena   Lubumbashi   MALAWI   Mahajanga
ANGOLA   Kitwe   Lilongwe   L. Nyasa   Nacala
Namibe   ZAMBIA   Lusaka   Antananarivo
L. Kariba   Harare   MOZAMBIQUE
NAMIBIA   ZIMBABWE   Beira   MADAGASCAR
Bulawayo   Toliara
Windhoek   BOTSWANA
Walvis Bay   Gaborone   Pretoria   Maputo
Luderitz   Johannesburg   Mbabane
SWAZILAND   Maputo
Maseru   Durban
LESOTHO
SOUTH AFRICA
Cape   Port
Town   Elizabeth

Indian Ocean

Africa

✪ National Capital
• City
- - - International Boundary
—— Rivers

0   Miles   100

The Heritage Library of African Peoples

WOLOF

Tijan M. Sallah, Ph.D.

THE ROSEN PUBLISHING GROUP, INC.
NEW YORK

For My In-Laws Mr. B. Haidara and Mrs. S. Tall.

Acknowledgment
When Ike Achebe asked me to participate as a writer in this project on the peoples of Africa taking a perspective "free from the Eurocentric bias of the past," I knew that he was following in the tradition of his celebrated father, Professor Chinua Achebe. I could not resist this worthwhile project. I knew that there was a need for outsiders to learn the truth about Africans, and for Africans to know each other better, but I wanted to write on an African people I knew. A few weeks later, Roger Rosen, the publisher, asked me to work on the Wolof of Senegal and Gambia. I am indeed grateful to both Roger and Ike for their encouragement and commitment to this noble enterprise.

I wish also to convey my thanks to Professor David P. Gamble. His books and many unpublished monographs on various aspects of Senegambian life deserve a Senegambian prize. I am also grateful to various sources I have consulted over the years in personal correspondence.

I wish particularly to thank my friend and Gambian compatriot, Professor Sulayman Nyang, Director of the African Studies Center at Howard University, who alerted me to sources that would have escaped my attention and who helped clarify some of my ideas on the Wolof.

Inevitably, much of this book draws heavily on what I learned growing up in an oral tradition. To the oral tradition, therefore, I owe my greatest intellectual debt. Any faults in this book, however, remain exclusively my responsibility.

Published in 1996 by The Rosen Publishing Group, Inc.
29 East 21st Street, New York, NY 10010

Copyright 1996 by The Rosen Publishing Group, Inc.

First Edition

Manufactured in the United States of America

Library of Congress Cataloging-in-Publication Data
Sallah, Tijan M., 1958–
    Wolof / Tijan M. Sallah.
      p.   cm. — (The heritage library of African peoples)
    Includes bibliographical references and index.
    ISBN 0–8239–1987–0
    1. Wolof (African people)—History—Juvenile literature. 2. Wolof (African people)—Social life and customs—Juvenile literature.
    [1. Wolof (African people)] I. Title. II. Series.
    DT509.45.W64S35 1996
    966.3'004963214—dc20   95-13328
                                         CIP
                                          AC

Contents

INTRODUCTION

THERE IS EVERY REASON FOR US TO KNOW
something about Africa and to understand its
past and the way of life of its peoples. Africa is a
rich continent that has for centuries provided
the world with art, culture, labor, wealth, and
natural resources. It has vast mineral deposits,
fossil fuels, and commercial crops.

But perhaps most important is the fact that
fossil evidence indicates that human beings
originated in Africa. The earliest traces of
human beings and their tools are almost two
million years old. Their descendants have
migrated throughout the world. To be human is
to be of African descent.

The experiences of the peoples who stayed in
Africa are as rich and as diverse as of those who
established themselves elsewhere. This series of
books describes their environment, their modes
of subsistence, their relationships, and their customs and beliefs. The books present the variety
of languages, histories, cultures, and religions
that are to be found on the African continent.
They demonstrate the historical linkages between
African peoples and the way contemporary Africa
has been affected by European colonial rule.

Africa is large, complex, and diverse. It en-
compasses an area of more than 11,700,000

square miles. The United States, Europe, and India could fit easily into it. The sheer size is an indication of the continent's great variety in geography, terrain, climate, flora, fauna, peoples, languages, and cultures.

Much of contemporary Africa has been shaped by European colonial rule, industrialization, urbanization, and the demands of a world economic system. For more than seventy years, large regions of Africa were ruled by Great Britain, France, Belgium, Portugal, and Spain. African peoples from various ethnic, linguistic, and cultural backgrounds were brought together to form colonial states.

For decades Africans struggled to gain their independence. It was not until after World War II that the colonial territories became independent African states. Today, almost all of Africa is ruled by Africans. Large numbers of Africans live in modern cities. Rural Africa is also being transformed, and yet its people still engage in many of their customs and beliefs.

Contemporary circumstances and natural events have not always been kind to ordinary Africans. Today, however, new popular social movements and technological innovations pose great promise for future development.

George C. Bond, Ph. D., Director
Institute of African Studies
Columbia University, New York

The Senegambian region of West Africa has a rich cultural heritage and also reflects many European and Muslim influences, as seen in this street scene in St. Louis, Senegal.

chapter

1

THE PEOPLE

THE WOLOF ARE A WEST AFRICAN PEOPLE with a reputation for wit and physical beauty. They live mostly in Senegal and the Gambia, a region called Senegambia. Their population today is over 5 million. They form more than half the population of Senegal and about 12 percent of the population of the Gambia.

The Wolof have preserved their ethnic identity as a result of their openness to other groups and peoples. For centuries they have lived side by side with the Serer, Mandinka, Fulani, Tukulors, and Jolas. They have traded goods and intermarried with these neighbors. Although they have fought neighbors in the past, today their relationship is one of tolerance and mutual jokes, which is known by the Wolof as *kal*. The Wolof accept any person who speaks their language and identifies with their customs. For this

FAMOUS WOLOF

Famous Wolof political figures are Blaise Diagne and Leopold Sedar Senghor. In 1914, Diagne became the first black African deputy in the French parliament. Senghor, whose origins are a blend of the Serer and Wolof ethnic groups, is a founder of the Negritude Movement and became first president of the Republic of Senegal. Later he was the first non-French member of the French Academy.

Cheikh Anta Diop is a famous Wolof historian, and physicist. Diop founded the Afrocentric movement, which traces many African origins back to ancient Egypt. He wrote many books arguing his view. He used carbon-dating techniques to present detailed evidence to support his arguments and illuminate how the history of Africa's peoples has been distorted. The Afrocentric Movement is very popular today among African-Americans. Diop popularized the view that Africans must look at their world not through Western eyes, but through their own. At the World Festival of Arts held in Dakar in 1966, Cheikh Anta Diop received an award along with the late African-American historian and philosopher W. E. B. DuBois, as the two people of African descent who had most influenced twentieth-century thought about people of African descent.

Other Wolof of world fame are Amadou Makhtar M'bow, who served as a Secretary General of the United Nations Educational, Scientific and Cultural Organization (UNESCO); Birago Diop, poet and veterinarian; Sembene Ousmane, writer and filmmaker popular for his themes of conflict between Senegalese tradition and modern forces; and Youssou Nolour, musician, known for his theatrical performances. Phillis Wheatley, the 18th-century Senegambian slave-poet who was taken to Boston, Massachusetts, and who became the founding mother of African-American literature, is alleged to have been Wolof. The Senegalese Wolof writer Aminata Sow Fall is known for her masterpiece depicting the plight of Senegalese beggars, *The Beggar's Strike.*

The land of the Wolof crosses the border between Senegal and Gambia, an area that is called Senegambia.

reason, the Wolof have expanded and include many crossovers with other groups. It is therefore difficult today for most Wolof to claim ethnic purity.

Unlike their Fulani neighbors, who are nomadic herders, the Wolof mostly live a life of settled agriculture, although some keep cattle. They inhabit mostly savanna grasslands in northwestern Senegal and in the territories on the north bank of the Gambia River. The soils in these areas are not fertile; they are usually sandy and dry.

Many Wolof today live in cities in Senegambia and other parts of the world. Urban Wolof in Senegambia live in houses made of mud or

Many African countries contain an interesting mix of rural life, which is frequently traditional, and modern cities. The Wolof joke about this difference in ways of life. This scene in St. Louis, Senegal, shows how the rural and urban coexist.

cement bricks and corrugated iron roofs. The rural Wolof live in houses of dried mud bricks with pyramid-shaped roofs made of dried palm fronds and grass. Roofs are often elaborately woven, and all the male family members participate in the installation.

Inside houses there is usually an iron or wooden bed, with a grass- or sponge-stuffed mattress and feather- or cotton-stuffed pillows. A clay jar filled with drinking water usually stands in a corner with a cover plate and a cup, from which all family members drink. Usually,

The Wolof are renowned throughout West Africa for their elegant dress. This woman is walking through the streets of St. Louis.

pictures of the family, living and dead, hang on the walls, and charms are placed on the windows and doors to protect against evil spirits.

Many Wolof are highly urbanized. They work as government civil servants, traders, or artisans and look down on rural Wolof and their rustic dialect as *faana faana*. Because of media influence, urbanized Wolof imitate every aspect of European and American life. The gap in living standards between the two branches of the Wolof is widening, but they bridge this gap with jokes and other aspects of *kal* relationships. City dwellers refer to the *faana faana* as *muuhat* (someone ignorant of modern ways; a rustic), and the latter refer to the urban Wolof as *toubab jakhateh* (carbon-copy whites) who are imitating western ways.

The Wolof are great storytellers. In family or village events, the young and old gather to listen. Stories often have a moral. Language is used with great skill by Wolof *griots*, or entertainers, who embellish stories with songs, gestures, and mimicry of both natural and supernatural characters. Wolof fables often identify particular traits with certain animals: cunning and wit with *Leuk*, the hare; thievery with *Bouki*, the hyena; gossip with *Choi*, the parrot; and courage with *Gayndeh*, the lion. Wolof stories also use supernatural creatures, such as *kouss*, the leprechauns; *konderong*, dwarfs with long beards; and *doma*, witches.

The Wolof are known throughout West Africa for their elegant clothes and delicious cuisine. On special occasions they dress in flowing robes with exquisite embroidery. A common West African dish that originated with the Wolof is *Jollof rice*. It consists of steamed rice cooked with meat or fish, vegetables, and oil, garnished with tomato paste, bay leaves, and garlic. The Wolof call it *benachin* (all in one dish).▲

2

THE SAVANNA

THE LAND OF THE WOLOF IS THE SAVANNA OF
Senegal and the Gambia. Dry and sandy plains
make up much of the savanna, with some parts
covered by tall elephant grass. The terrain is
mostly flat with some low, flat-topped hills.
Anthills protrude here and there.

Bird life is rich and colorful. Species include
finches, woodpeckers, sparrows, crows, vultures,
herons, owls, bushfowls, pigeons, and guinea
hens. Wolof boys sometimes use slingshots to
hunt birds for meat.

Species of trees dot the landscape: mango,
guava, orange, tangerine, grapefruit, mahogany,
oil palm, rubber, rosewood, coconut, pawpaw,
tamarind, and baobab. Apart from their fruits,
some of the trees supply charcoal and firewood,
construction timber, and wood for sculpture.

The rainy season is from July to October; the

rest of the year is hot and dry. Average rainfall is 12 to 39 inches per year.

▼ WOLOF SETTLEMENTS ▼

The rural villages of the Wolof are small, averaging 100 to 200 people, and usually about four miles apart. Settlements consist of a group of family compounds surrounding a family village center (*pencha*), where men gather to chat and discuss village matters, and travelers visit and relax. Drumming, dancing, feasts, and ceremonies take place in the *pencha*.

A family compound (*ker*) consists of a house or group of houses surrounded by a fence. In rural areas, the fence is made of dried palm fronds or millet or reed stalks; in urban areas, it is made of corrugated iron sheets, barbed wire, or cement walls. The compound head is referred to as *borom ker*.

▼ FARMING AMONG THE WOLOF ▼

Farm sizes average about 200 acres. Poor farmers mainly grow subsistence crops: kinds of millet and beans. Relatively wealthier farmers diversify with cash crops like cotton, groundnuts, sorghum, maize, and rice. After the harvest, seeds are stored on rooftops for use in the next planting season. Some are stored in pyramid-shaped silos made of woven palm fronds.

Long ago, when land was abundant, farmers

practiced shifting cultivation and slash-and-burn agriculture. In shifting cultivation the farmer uses a plot of land until the soil gets tired; then it is left alone to regain its fertility. In slash-and-burn agriculture, the bush on a new plot of land is cleared and burned. The ashes rapidly return nutrients to the soil.

The northern part of the savanna, called the Sahel, often suffers terrible droughts. Crops fail, herds die or have to be slaughtered, and people are threatened with starvation.

Now land is scarce, population is growing fast, and landless rural people must work for active farmers or migrate to cities in search of wage jobs. Those with land now have to farm the same plot over and over again. Such intensive farming requires more labor, farm inputs such as fertilizers, and better agricultural techniques. A few wealthy Wolof operate commercial farms, with tractors and other machinery. However, most rural Wolof still farm with traditional, hand-held tools and eat what they grow.

In the past, division of labor by gender and age was practiced in farming. Before the rainy season, young men did the hard work of clearing the bush and preparing the land for sowing. Once it rained and the seeds began to sprout, women and children weeded. Women also did most of the household chores of cooking, cleaning, childbearing, and childrearing. Today, how-

Today many Wolof women have jobs in urban areas. These women are at the flower market in Dakar.

Many Wolof give their livestock to Fulani to rear. Seen here is a cattle market at Rufisque, near Dakar.

ever, many Wolof women have jobs in villages, towns, and cities.

▼ LIVESTOCK ▼

Wolof families often own cattle, sheep, goats, and chickens. With cattle, the Wolof have developed a symbiotic relation with their Fulani neighbors, meaning that the groups cooperate. The Wolof give their stock to the Fulani to rear, and they collect manure from them for their farms, while the Fulani use the cows' milk. For important ceremonies, such as marriages or births, the Wolof often slaughter an ox and feast with their neighbors. Wolof women and children usually take care of the smaller animals.

Cattle generally are an important asset to the Wolof. They can easily be converted into cash when the occasion arises. Holding cattle allows heads of families to prepare for bridewealth payment and other important social obligations.▲

chapter

3

ORIGINS, HISTORY, AND RELIGION

SCHOLARS DO NOT AGREE ON THE ORIGINS OF the Wolof. Some believe they came from ancient Egypt, Yemen, or Libya. They cite similarities in language, culture, and spiritual practices and believe that the Wolof began their migration southward to Mauretania, Senegal, and Gambia as early as 525 BC.

Some historians argue that the Wolof are a hybrid ethnic group like other groups living near the edge of the Sahara Desert in the Sahel region. These historians believe that the Wolof are a mixture of groups including the Serers, Berbers, Jews, Arabs, Fulani, Mande, and Tukulors. Through migration, trade, and cultural exchanges with North Africa and the Mediterranean, the Wolof absorbed Judaic, Christian, and Islamic influences.

Some scholars trace the recent origins of the

Wolof to the historic Empire of Mali (not to be confused with the modern state of Mali), and consider the Wolof to be the western branch of the Songhay people.

Others argue that the Wolof are Serer who once lived in Mauretania, where ruins and fragments of pottery and ornaments resemble those of the Wolof today. They say the Wolof were driven southward from Mauretania to Senegal by Berber invaders. The Wolof today refer to Mauritania as *Ganarr*, derived from the Wolof words *gan* (visitor; stranger) and *narr* (Berber, Moor), suggesting that Mauretania was overtaken by visiting Berbers.

▼ ORAL HISTORY ▼

Going back to the 15th century, oral histories give many different versions of the story of Njajan Njai, founder of the Wolof Empire.

Some say that Njajan was the son of Abu Darday, an Almoravid conqueror who came from Mecca to preach Islam in Senegal. There he married the daughter of the Tukolor ruler. She became Njai's mother. Njajan took control of the Wolof kingdom of Waalo and later Jolof. Some say that Njajan Njai was a mysterious person of Fulani origin. Others say he was a Serer prince.

Most oral traditional accounts agree that Njajan emerged from the waters of a lake, pond, or stream in Waalo, along the River Senegal, to settle a dispute between fishermen from different villages. A few days later, the dispute occurred again, and Njajan emerged to settle it. The fishermen, impressed by Njajan's ability to bring order and justice, begged him to become their king. In this way Njajan founded the Jolof empire. Njai's descendants continued to rule many Wolof kingdoms. They combined their power and prestige until the French arrived in the 19th century.

The magical water origins of Njajan Njai suggest that royalty was considered divine among the Wolof. In crowning ceremonies, the king, the *buurba*, bathed in the Njasseu stream to symbolize descent from Njajan Njai.

The "golden ages" of the Wolof started with the legendary Njajan Njai in the 13th century. As the *buurba* of Jolof, he conquered the Wolof states of Waalo, Cayor, and Bawol and united them under his leadership. The Wolof empire later extended its control over the kingdoms of Sine and Saloum, which were predominantly Serer. The empire reached its peak in the 15th century, when it controlled much of Senegal and the north bank of the Gambia River.

▼ RELIGION ▼

Today the majority of Wolof in Senegambia identify themselves as Muslim, with a smaller

ISLAM

Islam is one of the great world religions. As a faith that believes in only one God, it shares traditions of the Bible with Judaism and Christianity. All the prophets of the Bible are respected by Muslims, but Muslims add Muhammad, the founder of their faith, as the last prophet. Islam is based on five pillars: the declaration and belief in one God (*tawheed*); five daily prayers (*salat*); giving alms to the poor (*zakat*); pilgrimage to the holy city of Mecca, the founding place of the faith, if one has the wealth and strength (*hajj*); and fasting in the month of Ramadan (*sawm*). The Sunni and Shi'ah are the two main denominations of Islam. The Sunni, orthodox Muslims, are the largest group. The Shi'ah, nonorthodox Muslims, comprise a minority of 10 percent of Muslims worldwide. They are followers of Ali, the cousin of Muhammad, and support his claim as the fourth caliph or ruler of Islam. Unlike the Sunni, who practice the basic Islamic beliefs of total submission to God, tolerance, and compassion for the less fortunate, the Shi'ah often harbor streaks of fundamentalism and rituals of self-whipping, which are condemned by the more peaceful Sunni.

number following Christianity. As in a great number of African cultures, however, aspects of traditional religion are fused with Islam or Christianity. Even among urbanized Wolof, many still regard the ancestors as important spiritual leaders of everyday life, although Allah or God is worshiped.

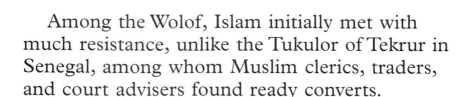

Among the Wolof, Islam initially met with much resistance, unlike the Tukulor of Tekrur in Senegal, among whom Muslim clerics, traders, and court advisers found ready converts.

The best description of Wolof religion might be a natural or traditional religion in which natural objects and phenomena such as thunder and lightning are agents of communion with higher spirits. People kept family deities and treated the earth and its fertility as the basis of their faith.

Wolof philosophy revolves around the human being (*nit*) and his or her relationships with society, nature, and the supernatural.

The Wolof see *nit* as a living bundle containing *hel* (mind/intelligence), *yaram* (body), *fit* (courage), and *sagoe* (will; that which balances the self). If any of these elements is absent or goes out of balance, a person is sick. Sickness is, therefore, a social and psychological imbalance, not only a physical one. This may explain why modern medicine alone sometimes does not solve medical problems for the Wolof, and they often go back to the traditional medicine-man (*jabran-kat*).

The *nit* operates in a social universe, and the Wolof put great emphasis on social belonging. In fact, they have a saying, *Nit nitai garabam* (a person is the medicine of another person). A person lives in a society, but one's social well-

Today most Wolof are Muslim. This is a view of worshipers in the court-yard of the Grand Mosque of Dakar.

being is linked to respecting and following community values. Perhaps the two most important values are *jom* (dignity, or self-respect) and self-knowledge (*ham-sa-bop*). The Wolof also value *ham-ham* (wisdom); *bakh* (goodness/kindness), *terranga* (hospitality), *dega* (honesty), *set* (cleanliness), *moun* (patience), *tegin* (good manners) *kersa* (respect for others), and *yaru* (discipline). A person's social rating is often linked to how well he or she respects these values.

A person must also respect the environment. The Wolof draw important lessons from nature. Largely an agricultural people, they recognize the importance of natural elements such as the

25

land, water, air, and fire in safeguarding their existence. The Wolof even have a saying that "The person who mistreats nature mistreats what benefits him."

In relations with the supernatural, the Wolof are much more guarded. Only special people possess powers to deal with the supernatural. First, there is the *doma* (witch), whom the Wolof see as possessing evil powers. Witches are very much feared. In earlier times, trials were held in which witches were summoned to declare before a public jury all the evil they had done. The spectacle of a witch speaking in tongues was known as *jaafur*.

Second, there is the *jinneh* (spirit), which can be good or bad and is believed to dwell sometimes in cotton trees. Spirits can descend to haunt people and influence their psychology. Good spirits provide protection, but evil spirits harm people. They cause madness, birth defects, and other deformities. Third, there is the *ninki-nanka* (supernatural dragonlike snake), awe of which is supposed to kill a person at first sight. It dwells in water and is believed to be covered with iridescent scales.▲

4

SOCIAL STRUCTURE

WOLOF SOCIETY WAS ORGANIZED INTO A hierarchy of castes, a rigid structure in which the social position of a person was inherited. A person's caste could not be changed, no matter what his or her merits. The Wolof caste system allowed members of the lower castes to achieve as much economic progress as the freeborn. In fact, many low castes were wealthier than their social superiors. Today, however, the caste system is giving way to a society based on merit and achievement.

The Wolof had three main castes: *jambur* or *gor* (freeborn), *nyenyo* (artisan castes), and *jam* (slaves).

▼ *JAMBUR* OR *GOR* ▼

The freeborn included both royalty and the poorest commoner (*baadola*). The main occupation of both was farming. Members of the royal lineage (*guelowar*) were at the top of the social pyramid. Succession to the throne was from the mother's side. Nobility was determined by relation to the royal lineages.

Women from the ruling families played significant roles in the Wolof states. They settled disputes affecting women, collected taxes, and sometimes assumed the throne. Women of royal lineage (queens, princesses) were known as *linguer*. The Wolof kings defined who they were in terms of the *linguer*. They were served by knights called *Samba linguer* (meaning "man of the *linguer*), who were known for their bravery and flamboyant generosity.

▼ NYENYO ▼

The *nyenyo* caste included the *tega* (goldsmiths, silversmiths, blacksmiths); *rabbakat* or *maabo* (weavers); *ude* (leather-workers); and the *gewel* (musicians, praise singers, and historians). These occupations were hereditary. Marriage outside of the caste was forbidden. A child born of a marriage between a *nyenyo* and a noble was known as a *sani*, which literally meant "someone thrown away."

The roles of the various castes enabled Wolof society to develop a rigid division of labor. The *tega* made weapons and farming tools. When guns were introduced, they repaired guns and

Wolof society was based on a strict hierarchy of castes. Today, however, Wolof have more social mobility. These men are Senegalese.

made bullets. Their skills at using the four elements of earth (ore), wind (air), fire, and water
made people ascribe supernatural powers to
them. The women of the *tega* often worked with
pottery and were skilled hairdressers.

The *rabbakat* (weavers) used handlooms and
other tools to make garments and fences. The
ude were the lowest category of the *nyenyo*, because working with animal hide was regarded as
unclean. They made shoes, amulet covers, bags,
mats, scabbards for knives, and harnesses for
horses.

The *gewel* or *griot* occupied a special place in
Wolof society. Every important family kept a
gewel, who was the family historian. The *gewel*
memorized family genealogies and advised on
lineage whenever royal succession was in ques-
tion. As important reservoirs of memory, *griots*
were used as court advisers to Wolof kings. The
gewel often provided entertainment at social
functions, such as play-acting, dancing, storytelling, and singing. At social events, the *gewel*
employed powers of flattery and praise to move
their patrons to shower gifts on them. In earlier
days, failure of a noble to meet this obligation
was often publicly ridiculed through the *gewel's*
powers of satire. Many *gewel* became wealthier
than their noble patrons, but intermarriage with
other castes was strictly prohibited.

The *gewel* had a reputation for drunkenness

The *gewel* or *griot* remains an important figure in Wolof society. He preserves oral history and provides music and entertainment. A *griot* such as this man continues Wolof traditions.

and indecent behavior. When they died, they were not buried in the earth, for it was believed that it would harm the crops. Instead, their bodies were deposited in the hollow trunks of baobab trees. Like *tega* women, *gewel* womenfolk were often hairdressers. Today the role of the *griot* has become increasingly commercialized so that facts and the powers of flattery are sometimes combined to confer cheap praise on the undeserved.

▼ *JAM* (SLAVES) ▼

The lowest category of people in the Wolof social pyramid were the slaves, but this caste increasingly declined during the 20th century.

31

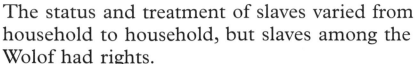

The status and treatment of slaves varied from household to household, but slaves among the Wolof had rights.

There were three categories of slaves: domestic (*jami-neg*), traded or captured (*jami-hareh*) and crown slaves (*jami-bur*). Domestic slaves born in the household were treated as junior members of the family and seldom sold. They were obliged to work for their master but were usually given their own land to farm and were allowed to marry and raise families. Trade slaves included those captured in war and could be bought and sold. Usually, they had no ties to the local community. Crown slaves usually did heavy manual labor for the king and state; however, crown slaves who were loyal and wise often became trusted advisers of the king. A special category of crown slaves were the *tyedo* or *ceddo* (warrior crown slaves). Warrior slaves were sometimes absorbed into the nobility when they demonstrated bravery and skill. Sometimes because of their power and wealth they played important roles in determining who would be the next king.▲

chapter

5

COLONIALISM AND RESISTANCE

THE PORTUGUESE WERE AMONG THE FIRST European explorers of the West African coast. Their arrival in 1444 in Senegambia began the growth of their maritime power in the area, and they began to trade with the Jolof Empire, flourishing after its consolidation by Njajan Njai. By this time, the Jolof Empire, with its capital in Warxox, had been Islamized. Its population was sparse; its economy was based on cattle, millet, slaves, horses, cloth, and trade with the Berbers of North Africa and the Mali Empire to the east.

During the 17th and 18th centuries, slaves and gum were Senegambia's main exports to Europe. Slaves from West Africa were needed to work in the plantations of the New World (the Americas and the West Indies). Generally, Senegambian rulers refrained from enslaving

Slavery had a great impact on the history of the Wolof. Seen here is the entrance to the slave jail on Gorée Island, now a museum.

their own subjects, but they sold into slavery prisoners captured in war. The European quest for slaves, however, increasingly shifted to the more densely populated areas of West and Central Africa.

The growth of the Atlantic slave trade increased competition for slaves in the local economy and caused warfare among rival kingdoms in the Senegambian region. Small farmers became victims of slave raids. Food production was disturbed, and famine and misery sometimes resulted. Growing warfare increased the power and size of the nobles and *tyedo* (warrior class), who victimized the farmers. As slavery and tension between the castes intensified in the

Many French married Wolof women, who became known as *signares*. Their descendants are found in *communes* in places such as Gorée Island, seen here.

region, a radical popular movement was born in 1673, led by Muslim clerics, *marabouts*, who revolted against the slave-trading aristocracy. The French collaborated with the traditional aristocracy to put down the revolt.

The French came to Senegal to benefit from the slave trade. They established bases on the island of N'Dar at Saint Louis in 1659 and drove the Dutch from the island of Gorée in 1677.

Before long the French intermarried with Wolof women. These women, the *signares*, were noted for their elegance of dress, stylish headwrap, dazzling jewelry, and other finery. The *signares* often had their own domestic slaves who mined gold for them. They also had musician-entertainers who sang praises to them. The offspring of the *signares* and the French became known as the métis (mulattoes, or Afro-French), who became powerful in the French colonial administration in Senegal. Today, many métis and their descendants are still found in Saint Louis, Gorée, and other French communities called *communes* in Senegal.

In Senegambia, Christianity was introduced through trade, missionary activity, and other exchanges. Because many Wolof were already Muslim, the few who became Christian were mostly descendants of *signares* and those who received Western education, which the Wolof called *jaangi nassarane* or Nazarene education (deriving from Jesus of Nazareth), because it was also seen as the path to Christianization. The Wolof who were associated with European trading activities became known as the *grumetes* (perhaps from the French, *gourmet*). The term is derived from European languages meaning "ship's boy" or "cabin boy" or "one who had a taste for food and other delights."

The French and the British became rivals for the Senegambia region. Although slaves were the main export from the region, the French and British traded horses, guns, guinea cloth, liquor and other European luxury goods to the Senegambians for salt, palm oil, and dried fish.

The French dominated Senegal and built their colonial system based on a "civilizing mission," which was to turn Africans into "black Europeans." This cultural policy was known as "assimilation." The British dominated the Gambia and carried out a colonial system based on "indirect rule," a policy of using traditional chiefs to rule in the rural back country.

▼ RESISTANCE ▼

French colonialism was widely resisted among the Wolof. The Tukulor, who were neighbors of the Wolof, had converted many Wolof and had pushed to establish Muslim theocratic states in the region. The most eminent of the Muslim clerical warriors was Al-Hajj Sheikh Umar Tall Al-Futiyu. Umar Tall was a Senegalese Tukulor from Gedeh in Futa Toro. He made the pilgrimage to Mecca in the 1820s and so impressed the Imam of Mecca with his scholarship that he was made Caliph of the western Sudan.

Umar Tall led a holy war and conquered Futa Jallon and the Bamana kingdoms of Karta and Segu. Attempting to extend his power into Senegal, he came into conflict with the French. Under Major Louis Faidherbe, governor of French Senegal, the French moved to stop

Umar Tall's westward expansion. Umar turned east to expand his empire over the Empire of Mali and was killed there in a battle in 1864 in the Dogon cliffs of Degembere.

Following the death of Umar Tall, one of his disciples, Ma Ba Diakho Ba, a Tukulor cleric, led a *jihad* (holy war) against the Mandinka chiefdoms on the banks of the Gambia River. Ma Ba's holy wars pitted the Muslim clerics (*marabouts*) against the traditional slave-trading nobility and *tyedo*. His forces took over Saloum and Jolof, and many prominent Wolof kings were converted to Islam.

The most prominent of these kings was Lat Jor Ngone Latir Jobe, the *Damel* (ruler) of Cayor. When the French ousted him as *Damel*, Lat Jor, confident in his new alliance with the powerful Ma Ba, raided Bawol and challenged French authority in the other Wolof states of Cayor, Jolof, and Sine.

Governor Faidherbe preferred Ma Ba to the traditional kings of Saloum because Ma Ba stopped the *tyedo* from pillaging the countryside and brought peace and stability that benefited agriculture and trade. However, Faidherbe could not allow Ma Ba to expand his *jihad* into areas of direct French interest. Ma Ba and the French signed a treaty of friendship that did not last long. French expansion in Senegal continued. Cayor was annexed. Lat Jor combined forces with Ma Ba and mounted a stiff resistance against the French.

Governor Faidherbe had installed a puppet regime, a government that was under his control, in Cayor headed by Lat Jor's relative, Majojo Jigen Kodu Fal. Lat Jor overthrew that government and forced the French governor to recognize him as *Damel*. Later he mounted strong resistance against the French all over the Wolof Empire. When the French insisted on a treaty to build a railroad through Cayor to facilitate trade, Lat Jor renounced the treaty and launched a rebellion, supported by his nephew, Samba Laobe, his allies Alboury Njai of Jollof and Abdul Bokar of Futa, and the Moors. But the French turned Samba Laobe against his uncle Lat Jor and appointed him *Damel*. At the battle of Dekele on the Bawol-Cayor border, Lat Jor was killed by the French along with his two sons and 18 warriors. The French governor is believed to have plotted the killing. Today, Lat Jor is immortalized in Wolof traditions as a national hero and a symbol of heroic resistance against European colonialism in Senegal.▲

The Wolof honor their artists and have rich traditions of art and literature. Wolof potters generally use red clay and decorate their ware with black and white designs.

chapter

6
LITERATURE AND ARTS

THE WOLOF HAVE A VERY STRONG TRADITION
of oral literature that reflects their history, philosophy, morality, and cultural expression.

▼ STORYTELLING ▼

A cherished Wolof art, daily storytelling
cements bonds between the different ages, gen-
ders, and castes of the listeners. The story (*leb*)
consists of six different genres. *Chosan* (historical
narrative) tells about the past, the deeds of he-
roes and antiheroes. The *lebatu* (proverbs) are
used to give point to a story and make it
memorable. The *chax* (riddles) are used to
strengthen the puzzle-solving skills of children.
Woi (songs) are used to entertain, mourn, or
mock, to spur emotional responses. Finally, the

WOLOF NJAI'S PROVERBS

Perhaps the most important source of Wolof wisdom are the sayings or proverbs attributed to Wolof Njai. Wolof Njai was not a real person but a fictional character believed to be the source of all Wolof wisdom. Some of his common proverbs follow:

A fowl that is carried on a person's shoulder has no sense of distance. (A person who is dependent may take for granted the burden carried by his helper.)

However long a log is in a river, it will not turn into a crocodile. (A foreigner can never turn into a native.)

A monkey is not ugly; it resembles the father. (A child is a product of his environment.)

Whoever wants honey should brave the bees. (In life good things come with risks.)

Do not burn the tree that bears the fruit. (Be selective in one's destruction.)

One who is afraid of the sun is afraid of what is of great benefit. (One should not be timid to take advantage of opportunity.)

One who resists human rule will be governed by the devil. (In life one has to obey the right authority.)

The fowl treads on its chickens but does not dislike them. (Parents punish their children but still love them.)

bida contain folk beliefs and combine all six genres. The gestures, sounds, and behavior of humans, animals, plants, and supernatural beings are imitated and presented in an entertaining manner. The audience often participates. Many of the stories are educational and contain a moral lesson. Stories often end with *"Fii la leb dohe tabi ajana"* (The story passed by here and entered heaven) or *"Fii la leb dohe tabi ca gech"* (The story passed by here and entered the river). This end to stories evokes their mysterious origin.

▼ POETRY ▼

There are five distinct types of poetry: *woi* (song); *taga* (praise poetry); *baaku* (praise challenge or war poetry); *kassak* (circumcision poetry); and *kebbetu* (rap poetry). A popular example of the *woi* is a lullaby with origins in the kingdom of Saloum:

> Father Malamin, religious teacher,
> Write me a talisman.
> Talismans are not easy to find in Saloum
> For Saloum is two houses.
>
> The third is a kitchen,
> And the kitchen belongs to the king.
> That king is the King of Saloum.
> Ayoo Ayai ya,
> Ayoo Baby,
> Little Baby crying.

This lullaby makes use of repetition, symbols, and facts from history. It refers to the 1300s when the kingdom of Saloum was divided into warring households. One part of the household held strongly to traditional Wolof religion, and the other embraced Islam. The King was faced with the difficult situation of a house divided between the old ways and the new.

The second type, the *taga*, employs flattery and exaggeration to praise a person who has rendered noble service to the society. An example of the *taga* is "*Samba Njai Ya Bakhone*," a praise poem for a dead person:

> Samba Njai was so good,
> The man with the three hearts.
> When Samba Njai died,
> Even the Europeans mourned.

The moral message is that people should follow Samba Njai's goodness and kindness.

The third form of Wolof poetry is the *baaku* or praise-challenge poetry, used to evoke the heroic in a wrestling contest or during war.

Kassak poetry is chanted only during the healing of the *njuli* (newly circumcised), who are taught many male secrets through riddles or coded puzzles called *passin*. Sexual education is taught through use of local images. The *kassak* "*Kopotoli*" illustrates this:

> Kopo toli, kopo toli
> Tolo li waii
> Grandfather's teeth have fallen;
> But his ax is still sharp.

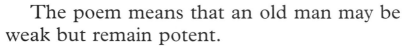

The poem means that an old man may be weak but remain potent.

Kebbetu, like rap poetry, has fast delivery, follows a call and response pattern, and employs repetition, street vulgarity, and local humor.

This poem mocks a young girl, Ndey Kumba, who carelessly got pregnant.

Call:	Ndey Kumba, what is wrong?
Response:	I am pregnant as a barrel.
Call:	I say, Ndey Kumba,
	What is wrong with you?
Response:	I say, I am pregnant as a barrel.
Call:	I say, Ndey Kumba,
	Who touched you?

The above show that Wolof poetry is varied and rich. Poetry and music are united in a single mission of entertainment and education. Poetry is sung and danced to, and its philosophical messages are appreciated and cherished.

▼ ART AND CRAFTS ▼

The Wolof are skilled craftspeople. Pottery, sculpture, weaving, and architecture are widely admired and important sources of income. Skilled craftspeople are often honored. Wolof pottery includes the large water jar (*ndal*) and the perforated incense burner (*anda*). Made of red clay baked in a traditional kiln, they are typically shaped like the number 8 with patterns

in charcoal black or chalk white. A pyramidal
cover fits over the mouth of pots. Other pottery
imitating natural shapes are used as decorative
pieces in Wolof households.

The art of woodcarving (*etta matta*) is highly
perfected among the Wolof. Mahogany and various types of wood in the immediate environs are
sculpted into human, animal, tree, and extra-
terrestrial forms to convey the wishes of the
carver. Sculptures are usually polished black or
brown and may be enhanced with ivory, cattle
tails and horns, pretty feathers, and other animal
items. In earlier days, both sculpture and pottery
played symbolic roles in Wolof religion.

The weaving of cloth, baskets, and fences is
integral to Wolof creative life. All are done by
hand, using simple tools. Beautiful cloth, coarse
or fine, is produced on a handloom using a
shuttle. Cool cotton cloth, whether hand-made
or mass produced, often has elaborate geometric
and organic motifs. Baskets and fences are usually woven from palm fronds.

Rural Wolof architecture values beauty together with stability, hygiene, and social unity.
In a typical village, a family would have a mud
house (usually of geometric shape) known as a
neg. The kitchen (*wayng*), because it burns
firewood or charcoal for cooking, is separated
from the house for health reasons. For the same
reasons, deep pit toilets (*kama*) are separated

Today many Wolof artists sell to tourists and international collectors. At this craft village outside Dakar artists are trained and sell their work to visitors.

and placed far from wells to avoid groundwater pollution. Storage facilities (*pukus*) for food, prone to infestation by pests such as mice and ants, are separated from the house and sometimes attached to the kitchen. Family compounds are separated by a reed fence and fruit and other ornamental trees. Shady compound courtyards are used for household activities such as pounding grain, washing clothes, and smoking fish. In the overall design of a village, social unity is key; hence families situate as close to each other as possible to support each other in case of adversity.▲

47

chapter

7

CUSTOMS

▼ NAMING CEREMONY ▼

The naming ceremony (*ngenteh*) of a newborn child takes place on the seventh day after birth. It is heavily influenced by Islamic teachings. On the naming day, the child's head is shaved and the child is given a name. A sheep, goat, or chicken is sacrificed, depending on the wealth of the parents. Friends and relatives bring gifts, which the parents in turn give to the *nyenyos* (musicians, gold/blacksmiths, and leather workers).

Usually, the mother is ceremoniously washed early in the morning, and she wears her best clothes for the naming occasion. The baby is brought out wrapped in white cloth, and while the head is being shaved, the call to prayer is whispered into its ear. Kolanuts are broken and

Wolof children play together until they begin to take on gender roles that often follow their parents' occupations. These children are sitting on beautifully painted fishing boats.

shared, and pancakes and millet porridge are eaten to commemorate the occasion.

▼ CHILD DEVELOPMENT ▼

The Wolof value children greatly. A child (*dom*) is seen as a neighborhood property, so child care is jointly exercised. A child is taught good values and etiquette. The child should greet elders, help parents with household work, avoid foul language, and listen to the wisdom of elders. In early life, boys and girls play together. As they grow, gender roles become more sharply defined, but their intelligence is understood to be equal.

Today many Wolof women are professional traders. This woman's vegetable display is typical of the artistic attention given to laying out items for sale.

Among the many forms of recreation enjoyed in Senegambia is boat racing.

▼ DAILY LIFE ▼

The day starts among the Wolof with greetings. Young men often shake hands and young women curtsy when they greet elders. They ask, "*Jama nga am?*" (Do you have peace?), and the response is, "*Jama rek*" (Peace only is what I have). Then inquiries follow about everyone in the household.

After greetings, in rural areas, a person often takes a shower with a bucket of water. In the cities, modern showers are common. People then eat breakfast of *rui* (pap), *churra* (porridge), or fried foods such as *akara* (fried bean flower), *yokhos* (fried oyster) or *jen* (fried fish). People then head to work. In the rural areas, the main work is farming. In the urban areas, occupations are similar to those in any modern city, but there are many traders. Lunch usually consists of steamed rice, millet, or couscous with a tasty stew of vegetables, nuts, or meat.

51

Recreation follows work. People may sit, chat, and enjoy each other's company with stories and sharing of news. They may attend a wrestling match or, nowadays, watch or play soccer, basketball, or cricket. Some people go to the sea or river to swim, fish, and ride boats.

In the evening, people eat supper, enjoy each other's company, and then retire to sleep. If dreams occur during the night, it is common to share them with one's immediate family the next day. Dreams are considered meaningful, and some people have the power to interpret them and provide meaningful advice.

▼ INITIATION ▼

Wolof boys go through an initiation school as part of the process of reaching maturity. The group of initiates are ceremonially circumcised during initiation. Newly circumcised boys (*njuli*) are ritually secluded in one large room known as *mbarr* (shop). Only adults and sometimes elderly women are allowed to visit the *mbarr*. The boys are drilled in special songs (*kassak*) and sexual puzzles (*passin*) by men who act as guardians (*salbeh*). The guardians quiz the *njuli*, punishing with a cane when one misses the meaning of a puzzle. To the Wolof, maturity means the ability to withstand pain and suffering. At the end of the circumcision, the initiates are welcomed to a huge festival known as *samba sokho*.

Wolof boys generally undergo initiation during which they assimilate many traditional values. In addition, they attend school and learn to write Arabic and read the Koran. Washable boards are used for writing (below). There is also time to relax (top).

▼ MARRIAGE ▼

Marriage is the mark of true maturity. In rural areas, parents often arrange marriages for their children. A young man may want a young woman, but his father decides whether she is suitable. A go-between is often appointed to do detective work about the woman's family background. If the father finds the family satisfactory, he sends the go-between to deliver kolanuts to the woman's parents. The parents accept the kolanuts if they approve of the young man.

Marriage is called *taka,* which literally means "tying the knot." Since the coming of Islam, most marriages are conducted at the mosque. The father of the groom pays the bridewealth to the young woman's father and also to the *imam* (religious leader) performing the marriage. The bride moves to the groom's house with great ceremony. Relatives and friends drum, sing, and dance. Young women sing ribald songs (*woyi sait*) to provoke and entertain. Usually, many days of festivities follow.

Polygyny, or one man having more than one wife, is practiced by men, but polyandry, a woman's having more than one husband, is forbidden. Having several wives is usually an indication of status and wealth. In rural areas, a large family provided many hands to work on the farms and expand the family's wealth. Polygyny is now on the decline, especially in urban areas but also in rural areas.

▼ DEATH ▼

Among the Wolof, death is a path by which one joins the ancestors. When a person dies, loud mournings echo from the house of the bereaved. Neighbors stop by to help. Relatives and friends are informed of the death and summoned to attend the funeral. The body is washed, perfumed, and wrapped in a shroud of white cloth. Men prepare the bodies of males, and women those of females.

The body is allowed to stay in the house only for about two days. It is placed on a stretcher, and group prayers are performed following the Muslim pattern. Only men participate at this stage. When the body is buried at the graveyard, prayers are said again. Participants then turn away, never looking back. Usually, a person is buried near relatives for company. If a person can afford it, a tombstone is erected. Relatives return annually to place wreaths and to say prayers.

On the third day after the burial, a major charity event is held, including a feast for relatives, neighbors, and the poor. Kolanuts are broken, and prayers are said for the person who died.▲

8

THE FUTURE

THROUGHOUT THEIR HISTORY, THE WOLOF have shown remarkable initiative and adaptability to changing circumstances. They have influenced other Africans, Europeans, and Middle Easterners with whom they came into contact and have also been influenced by them. Through their openness, they have shared techniques, ideas, and resources with outsiders. This has enabled them to exercise leadership roles in the government, agriculture, business, and trade of the Senegambia region.

Social change has been rapid in the past 30 years. With political independence came the development of political parties, greater educational facilities, improvements in health services and communication, and the growth of cities. The Wolof have played active roles in every sector of Senegambian life. In politics, for example, they hold a fair share of cabinet posts.

The Wolof view of the future is optimistic, recognizing and willing to accept the challenges of change in the contemporary fields of culture, science, technology, and business.

In business, Wolof traders (*bana-bana*) are known for their bargaining skill and thrift in places as diverse as Abidjan, Ivory Coast; Casablanca, Morocco; Paris, France; Rome, Italy; and New York City. They develop networks and share living costs by living in groups in a single apartment. Wolof street vendors sell merchandise at home and worldwide. Despite strict immigration laws abroad and barriers of race, language, and culture, Wolof merchants are able to overcome great odds and make profits even in poor communities.

Wolof society is undergoing significant change. The caste system, for example, is slowly giving way to a society based on merit. Intercaste marriages have increased, and many people who came from the lower castes now occupy high positions in government and business.

The pressures of modern economics are also being felt in the Wolof extended family. The cost of living has risen. The old safety nets provided by the large family are disappearing. Young couples now prefer fewer children. Unlike elsewhere in the world, Wolof women have always participated in economic activity outside the household. Today, they hold jobs in government and in the private sector. As in the past, today they organize small enterprises, such as cloth dyeing, sewing, and farming, and employ men and women to work for them.

Now Wolof women and men drive cars, own television sets, work in air-conditioned offices, operate computers, and travel and trade internationally. The Wolof have adapted well to modernity. Their view of the future is similar to that of the rest of the modern world. But as the future arrives, age-old customs and traditions are dying. Wolof parents have begun to feel the vices of modernity taking over. Prostitution, materialism, crime, drugs, atheism, and erosion of social values are becoming common in large cities. Like peoples the world over, the Wolof are learning to cope with the challenges of the modern world. They want to preserve what was good in the past and be open to the challenges of the future.▲

Glossary

bana-bana Wolof traders.

borom ker Owner of a compound.

bridewealth Money and/or goods given to the bride's family by the groom's family.

buurba Wolof king.

Damel King of Cayor.

dom Child.

doma Witch.

faana-faana Rural or rustic Wolof.

fundamentalism Act of taking a belief to extremes.

genealogy Descent, as a person or family, from an ancestor or ancestors.

genre Artistic works that have the same form or style.

gewel or griot Member of the class of musicians, poets, and entertainers who also record oral history.

guelowar Royalty; noble from the royal lineage.

jabran-kat Practitioner of traditional medicine; medicine-man.

jam Slave.

jambur or gor Freeborn.

jinneh A good or bad spirit.

ker Compound; a piece of real estate.

konderong Dwarf.

kouss Leprechaun.

kal Joking relationship.

leb Story.

linguer Women of royal lineage; princesses and queens.

marabouts Muslim clerics.

nit A human being.

njuli Newly circumcised.

nyenyo Artisan castes.

pencha The village center.

samba linguer Knight.

signares Wolof women who married to French men and began commercial enterprises.

taka Marriage; literally "tying the knot."

tyedo Warrior crown-slave.

woi Song; poetry.

For Further Reading

Charles, Eunice A. *Precolonial Senegal: The Jolof Kingdom, 1800–1890.* Boston University, African Studies Center: African Research Studies, Number 12, 1977.

Colvin, Lucie Gallistel. *Historical Dictionary of Senegal.* Metuchen, NJ: The Scarecrow Press, Inc., 1981.

Gailey, Harry A. *A History of the Gambia.* London: Routledge & Kegan Paul, 1964.

Gamble, David P. *The Wolof of Senegambia: Together with Notes on the Lebu and the Serer.* London: International African Institute, 1957.

Magel, Emil A. *Folktales from the Gambia: Wolof Fictional Narratives.* Washington, DC: Three Continents Press, 1984.

Mahoney, Florence. *Stories of the Gambia.* Banjul, The Gambia: The Government Printer, 1975.

Sallah, Tijan M. "Phillis Wheatley: a brief survey of the life and works of a Gambian slave/poet in New England America." In *Wasafiri*, Association for the Teaching of Caribbean, African, Asian and Associated Literatures, University of Kent, Canterbury, No. 15, Spring, 1992, pp. 27–31.

Index

About the Author

Tijan M. Sallah is an economist and a celebrated Gambian poet and short-story writer. He was born in Sere Kunda, The Gambia, where he spent his early youth and graduated from St. Augustine's High School. He did undergraduate work at Berea College and received a Ph.D. in economics at Virginia Polytechnic Institute. In addition to being a professor of economics at several American universities, he has published many articles on economics, politics, literary criticism, and creative literature.

Dr. Sallah's books include: *When Africa Was a Young Woman* (poems, 1980), *Before the New Earth* (short stories, 1988), *Kora Land* (poems, 1989), and *Dreams of Dusty Roads* (poems, 1993). He has edited an anthology, *New Poets of West Africa*, forthcoming, and his works have appeared in several established anthologies, including Chinua Achebe and C.L. Innes's *The Heinemann Book of Contemporary African Short Stories*.

Photo Credits

Cover and pp. 31, 50, 51 © Michel Renaudeau/Gamma Liaison International; pp. 8, 12, 13, 29, 35, 49, 53 © Eric L. Wheater, New York; p. 18 top © Wolfgang Kaehler/Gamma Liaison International; p. 34 © Findlay Kembeu/Royal Geographical Society; p. 18 bottom © United Nations/A. Hozberg; pp. 25, 40, 47 © United Nations.

Editor

Gary van Wyk, Ph.D.

Design

Kim Sonsky